20

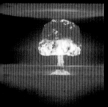

MONUMENTAL MILESTONES
GREAT EVENTS OF MODERN TIMES

The Fall of the Berlin Wall

On November 11, 1989, the fall of the Berlin Wall started taking place.

Mitchell Lane
PUBLISHERS

P.O. Box 196
Hockessin, Delaware 19707

Titles in the Series

MONUMENTAL MILESTONES
GREAT EVENTS OF MODERN TIMES

The Fall of the Berlin Wall

On November 11, 1989, the fall of the Berlin Wall started taking place.

Kathleen Tracy

Copyright © 2005 by Mitchell Lane Publishers, Inc. All rights reserved. No part of this book may be reproduced without written permission from the publisher.
Printed and bound in the United States of America.
Printing   1   2   3   4   5   6   7   8

Library of Congress Cataloging-in-Publication Data
Tracy, Kathleen.
    The fall of the Berlin Wall / by Kathleen Tracy.
        p. cm. — (Monumental milestones)
    Includes bibliographical references and index.
    ISBN 1-58415-405-5 (library bound)
    1. Berlin Wall, Berlin, Germany, 1961–1989—Juvenile literature. 2. Berlin (Germany)—Politics and government—1945–1990—Juvenile literature. 3. Germany—History—Unification, 1990—Juvenile literature. 4. Cold War—Juvenile literature. I. Title. II. Series.
    DD881.T74 2005
    943'.155087—dc22

                                                             2004030262

ABOUT THE AUTHOR: Kathleen Tracy has been a journalist for over twenty years. Her writing has been featured in magazines including *The Toronto Star*'s "Star Week," *A Biography* magazine, *KidScreen* and *TV Times*. She is also the author of numerous biographies including, *The Boy Who Would be King* (Dutton), *Jerry Seinfeld—The Entire Domain* (Carol Publishing), *Don Imus—America's Cowboy* (Carroll), *Mariano Guadalupe Vallejo*, and *William Hewlett: Pioneer of the Computer Age* both for Mitchell Lane. Also for Mitchell Lane, she wrote *Top Secret: The Story of the Manhattan Project* and *Henry Bessemer: Making Steel from Iron*. She recently completed *Diana Rigg: The Biography* for Benbella Books.

PHOTO CREDITS: Cover, pp. 1, 3—AFP/Getty Images; p. 6—Hulton Archive/Getty Images; pp. 12, 14, 15, 18, 20, 23, 25, 28, 30, 32, 39—Library of Congress; p. 26—Sharon Beck; pp. 10, 34, 36, 41—Sean Doughtery.

PUBLISHER'S NOTE: This story is based on the author's extensive research, which he believes to be accurate. Documentation of such research is contained on page 47.

The internet sites referenced herein were active as of the publication date. Due to the fleeting nature of some web sites, we cannot guarantee they will all be active when you are reading this book.

Contents

The Fall of the Berlin Wall

Kathleen Tracy

*For Your Information

A woman trying to escape East Germany.

In the months following the construction of the Berlin Wall, it was still fairly easy and safe to cross the border from East to West Berlin. But so many people successfully escaped that the East German government issued shoot to kill orders. From that point on, more than one thousand people would lose their lives trying to cross the Wall.

CHAPTER 1

The Quest for Freedom

While the Berlin Wall—the wall that literally cut the German capital city in half—may have been the most famous symbol of political oppression in the latter half of the twentieth century, it was also the greatest symbol of the human desire to live in freedom. Thousands of people risked death sneaking across the wall to reach the safety and freedom of West Berlin and devised many ways to do it.

In the years after the Berlin Wall was built, a network of tunnels were dug, mostly by college students who burrowed under the wall to gain freedom. Unfortunately, the tunnels were discovered after a woman left her baby's carriage near the opening of one. East German officials quickly closed them off.

Two families, the Wetzyls and Strzycks, actually attempted to fly over the wall. Over the course of many months they bought small amounts of nylon. If they had bought a huge roll of nylon it would have raised the suspicions of authorities so they patiently amassed the cloth strip by strip. When they finally had enough, they sewed it together and made a hot air balloon. The families got into the balloon's basket and after two nerve-wracking hours finally floated far enough over the wall to land in West Berlin. When news of their successful escape was made public, the East German government was so upset it restricted the sale of all lightweight cloth.

The most popular way to escape was to make a run for it and simply climb over the wall. At first, it was fairly easy to climb the wall.

But so many people were successful that East Berlin outlawed the sale of all rope. The government also increased the number of guards patrolling the wall and issued a shoot to kill order. The first person killed trying to cross the wall was Günter Litwin, who was shot to death in August 1961. After that, anyone trying to escape knew he or she was literally facing death. But for many, like Chris Gueffroy, it was a risk they were willing to take for the chance to be free.

All Gueffroy had known growing up was the repression of living under the rigid rules and regulations of communist East Germany. His divorced mom, Karin, who had raised Chris and his older brother Stefan alone, had long ago accepted life in East Berlin. But Chris felt increasingly like a prisoner as he grew older.

Karin would recall in an interview with NBC news that, "At age 12 or 13, Chris watched political TV shows from the west and always told me that one day, he will travel to America, his dream country. I was startled by his remarks and replied that he will not be able to leave East Germany, that it will never work." Her son refused to accept it and the dream to be free grew stronger. Karin added, "The mid-eighties were a time when many people left. I remember that we had to say farewell to a good friend of ours. After Chris had brought her to the door, he was angry, asking me why we [were] not leaving. Chris even called me a coward, said that he did not want to accept this lifestyle for the rest of his life. But he never talked about escaping or leaving the eastern part of Berlin."[1]

But that was exactly what he planned to do. His mother never dreamed that her son would try something so dangerous but on February 6, 1989, Gueffroy, 20, and his friend Christian Gaudian put their plan in motion. Uppermost in their minds was their belief that the shoot-to-kill order had been lifted. Around midnight, they quietly approached the wall and climbed over a steel fence. Suddenly, alarms went off. Guards came running over, firing their weapons. Gaudian was shot in the foot

and captured. Chris was hit ten times, including once through the heart and died on the spot. In a terrible irony, Karin, who lived only a few miles from the wall, had been awake reading and heard the gunfire, never suspecting it was her son being shot.

But the next day, after her son didn't show up for a planned visit, Karin began to suspect the terrible truth. For two agonizing days she worried and waited. What she didn't know was that East German officials had placed her under secret surveillance to see if she was also planning to escape or to help others escape. Eventually, she was taken in for questioning by the East German secret police, the Stasi. Finally, they told her that Chris had been killed while participating in an attack on a military facility. His friend had been wounded but survived, was in custody and would eventually be sentenced to three years in prison for illegal border crossing.

For several weeks after Chris' death, Karin was regularly questioned. In the end, the East German authorities determined Chris' shooting was justified because he was a criminal

Nine months later, the Berlin Wall fell, giving all East Germans the freedom Chris died trying to find. Geuffroy holds the tragic distinction of being the last person killed trying to cross the Berlin Wall.

The four guards involved in Gueffroy's shooting were at first hailed as heroes by East Germany. They received medals and a cash reward. However, after the reunification of Germany, they were put on trial in Berlin. Two were eventually released and another received a suspended sentence. The fourth, Ingo Heinrich, who, it was determined, fired the shot through Chris' heart, was found responsible for wrongfully causing Gueffroy's death and sentenced to three and a half years in prison, which was later reduced to two years of probation.

In all, over 5,000 people successfully escaped East Berlin between August 13, 1961 and November 9, 1989. In that same time span, 1,065 people were killed trying to cross the East German Border. On

what would have been his 35th birthday, June 21, 2003, the city of Berlin dedicated a monument in the honor of Chris Gueffroy, the last person killed attempting to climb the Berlin Wall in search of freedom.

The Berlin Wall stood from 1961 to 1989.

Although 5,000 people safely escaped over the Berlin Wall, over 1,000 died. Just nine months before the Wall was torn down, twenty-year-old Chris Gueffroy was shot to death. After the reunification of Germany, the guard responsible for his death was convicted of wrongfully causing his death. Today there is a memorial in Berlin honoring Gueffroy as the last person killed trying to climb the Berlin Wall.

FOR YOUR INFORMATION

For twenty-eight years the Berlin Wall was the ultimate symbol of political oppression. It separated friends and families and held half a city hostage. Although East Germans were prevented from leaving, non-Germans were allowed to pass back and forth between East and West Berlin through several Allied checkpoints. The checkpoints were named using military slang for letters of the alphabet—alpha, bravo, and Charlie, delta, etc. The most famous of the checkpoints was the third, Checkpoint Charlie, located at the intersection of Friedrichstrasse and Zimmerstrasse. Most of the people traveling between the two Berlins used this gateway.

After the Cuban Missile crisis had brought the world to the brink of nuclear war, the United States government stationed tanks and troops at Checkpoint Charlie to ensure that there would be no attempt to attack West Berlin. Nearly a year later, Peter Fechter was shot by East German guards near Checkpoint Charlie as he tried to escape and was left to bleed to death.

In 1989, the people of East Germany revolted and succeeded in tearing down the Berlin Wall. At Checkpoint Charlie, people were given glasses of champagne as they crossed into West Germany. A short time later, the original guard house was removed, but in 2001, a replica was built on the site as a memorial. Since then, a museum was built at Checkpoint Charley that has become a popular tourist destination.

However, in 2004 a controversy erupted over the site of Checkpoint Charlie. The owner of the museum built a reconstruction of the wall as part of its display, along with 1,065 crosses commemorating the people who were killed trying to escape the former East Germany. But a court ruled that the display must be taken down to make way for a proposed old-German Village theme-park.

Soviet leader Joseph Stalin and President Franklin Roosevelt were uneasy allies during World War II.

In the effort to stop Hitler from conquering all of Europe, the United States and the Soviet Union were allies during World War II. But as soon as the war ended, the two super powers started a "cold war" that pitted democracy against communism. The tensions between the two countries would directly lead to the establishment of the Berlin Wall.

Rebuilding

Even before Germany officially surrendered to end the European campaign in World War II, the Allied leaders were discussing what should happen to the country. In February 1945, President Franklin Delano Roosevelt met with Britain's Winston Churchill and Soviet leader Joseph Stalin. The meeting was held in Yalta, located in Crimea in the U.S.S.R.

During these top secret discussions, it was tentatively decided that only an unconditional surrender would be accepted from Germany, and that a trial for war crimes would be conducted. In addition, plans were laid to divide post-war Germany into four zones, each of which would be occupied by one of the four major Allies—Britain, France, the United States, and the Soviets. In addition Berlin, the German capital, would also be jointly controlled by the Allies.

Both Churchill and Roosevelt tried to limit the Soviet post-war influence in Eastern Europe. With Soviet troops already stationed throughout the region, the U.S.S.R. was already poised to exert control. The only concession Stalin would give was to promise free elections would be held. But Stalin resisted promoting democracy, claiming that the only way to ensure the U.S.S.R.'s safety was to surround it with like-minded communist countries.

Roosevelt was aware that for the time being, Stalin had the upper hand.

But Roosevelt believed that the soon-to-convene United Nations would be better able to control Stalin. France and China were also invited

Britain's Winston Churchill sought to limit Soviet influence in Eastern Europe.

Prior to the end of World War II, the four primary Allied Countries—the United States, France, Britain, and the Soviet Union—secretly met in Yalta and agreed post-War Germany and its capital city Berlin, would be divided into four zones that would each be controlled by one of the major Allies.

to co-sponsor the U.N.'s first gathering, which was scheduled for San Francisco on April 25 of that year.

On May 7, 1945, Germany officially surrendered and the next day was proclaimed VE Day: Victory in Europe. Two months later, Allied leaders met again in the German city of Potsdam to publicly confirm what had been secretly decided in Yalta. This time the U.S. was represented by President Harry Truman, who had taken office after Roosevelt's death less than two months after the Yalta conference.

Although China, Britain, and the United States were able to come to terms on issues surrounding the expected eventual surrender of Japan, the issues surrounding Europe had grown less clear. Of particular concern to the Western Allies in general and the United States in particular

was the awareness that communism was gaining support in Eastern Europe—and that the Soviets appeared ready to use that to its post-war advantage. One of Truman's main objectives at Potsdam was to ensure democracy would remain strong in Western Europe. The President had unique leverage over the Soviets—America was the only country in the world that possessed the atomic bomb.

In a memoir, Truman would later recall, "On July 24 I casually mentioned to Stalin that we had a new weapon of unusual destructive force. The Russian Premier showed no special interest. All he said was he was glad to hear it and hoped we would make 'good use of it against the Japanese.'" Even though Stalin didn't outwardly react to the news, Truman's admission would dictate Soviet policy for the next half century.[1]

The news of Germany's unconditional surrender was greeted by wild celebrations in the United States. Although it signaled the end of fighting in Europe, the war in the Pacific would continue until the United States dropped an atom bomb on Japan three months later.

On May 7, 1945, Germany surrendered and the next day was declared VE Day.

Over the course of a week, the Potsdam Agreement was worked out. It repeated the plan to divide Germany and Berlin into four zones. These would be controlled by the United States, Great Britain, France, and the Soviet Union. The Allies outlawed National Socialism, or Nazism, and disarmed Germany so that it could not be a military power. Instead, the foundation for a democratic government would be laid and various agricultural and business programs would be established to help rebuild the country's economy. Finally, it was agreed that an Allied Control Council made up of representatives from the four major Allies would confer over anything to do with Germany so that a consensus, or agreement, could be made over issues that would arise in the future.

The reason the Allies were so determined to keep control over Germany was its past history of military aggression. Up until late in the 1800s, the area now known as Germany was comprised of several independent states loosely aligned together. It wasn't until 1871 that the states were unified under one national flag. But from its beginning, Germany was consumed by a desire to expand its influence. The German government felt it was necessary to be considered equal to other European powers. So when Austria-Hungary went to war with Russia, Germany joined the fight. What began as a regional conflict eventually grew into World War I. Much to the country's surprise, Germany was soundly defeated and was forced to surrender in November 1918.

After the humiliating defeat, an effort was made to establish a British-styled parliamentary democracy in Germany. But Germans, embittered by their military loss, did not support the new government. The worldwide Great Depression of the early 1930s made Germany more open to extreme politicians who promised to restore Germany to its former glory. One politician in particular struck a chord with Germans and, in 1933, Adolf Hitler was named German Chancellor.

Within two years, Hitler and his Socialist German Workers' Party had removed all his political opponents and turned Germany into a totalitarian state under his complete control. For the next five years,

Germany's economy flourished under Hitler who intended to make Germany the supreme ruler of all Europe. The cornerstone of Hitler's vision was his belief in German—or Aryan, as he mistakenly called it—supremacy over other ethnic cultures, which included all minorities, especially Jews. He even ordered that all German athletic organizations become "Aryan only," so that only "perfect" specimens of the "Master Race" would ever represent Germany in international competitions, such as the Olympics.

In 1939, Hitler invaded Poland, which signaled the start of World War II. Although Hitler was eventually defeated, it came with a horrifying cost. Millions of civilians and soldiers died, including over six million Jews who were murdered in concentration camps, during the six year-conflict. Major European cities suffered catastrophic devastation including Berlin and London. That is why Allied leaders were so determined to keep a tight rein on Germany with one hand while with the other it tried to rebuild the country with democratic ideals.

Besides being the German capital, Berlin had been an important European city from the time it was established as a central trading post in the 13th century. In 1470, the local Prince, Friedrich II of Brandenburg, moved to Berlin and built a royal palace. Ironically, in the 17th century, the ruler Friedrich Wilhelm encouraged Jewish settlers looking for religious freedom to come to Berlin where they would be allowed to worship in peace. Wilhelm's son, Friedrich I, the first Prussian King, named Berlin his capital. He encouraged the development of arts and sciences and the city soon became a cultural center as well as a vital industrial powerhouse. It had an estimated population of two million people by the turn of the twentieth century.

Allied bombing during World War II left much of the city in ruin, but the Allies were determined to rebuild the city, in part to win over the German people and make them more open to democracy. But the good intentions of the Potsdam Agreement never quite worked out that way. The agreement to divide Berlin equally among the Allies had put that

capital in a strange situation. It was now isolated within the Soviet zone. Almost immediately, disagreements arose among the Allies and Berlin became a lightening rod for the escalating tensions. Soon the dream of a unified Germany fell apart as democracy and communism squared off in a new, undeclared war.

Adolf Hitler promised to restore Germany to its former glory. . . .

. . . by having the German "Master Race" conquer all of Europe. Hitler believed Germans were inherently superior to other ethnic cultures, particularly Jews. More than six million Jews died or were murdered in concentration camps as part of his "final solution."

FOR YOUR INFORMATION

Although the Olympic Committee awarded the city of Berlin the 1936 Summer Games before the Nazi Party came to power, the timing could not have been more perfect for Adolf Hitler. He saw the revered sports competition as the perfect place to showcase Aryan superiority to the world.

Hitler also made sure his true politics were hidden so that Germany was seen as a forward thinking, tolerant country. He ordered the removal of anti-Jewish signs and saw to it that newspapers did not run blatantly anti-Jewish stories during the time that foreign tourists and journalists were in Berlin for the Olympics. He went to these lengths because Jewish organizations in several countries had tried to pressure their governments to boycott the Olympics as a protest against the harsh Nazi policies towards Jews. But once the United States officially rejected the idea of a boycott, so did the other countries in Europe.

**Naoto Tajima, Jesee Owens,
and Luz Long**

More athletes participated in Berlin than ever had before, with Germany fielding the largest team of 348 athletes. The United States team was second with 312. The star of the German team was a track and field athlete named Luz Long. Long perfectly reflected Hitler's Aryan ideal, with blond hair, blue eyes, and chiseled features. However, the most famous athlete in the world at that time was American Jesse Owens, an African American from Alabama. Because Owens was black, Hitler considered him inferior and was anxious for Long to prove it.

It didn't work out that way. The "racially inferior" Owens would go on to win four gold medals at the Berlin Olympics: in the 100 and 200 meter races, in the 4 x 100 relay *and* the long jump. Interestingly, Long was the first person to congratulate Owens when the competition was over. An enraged Hitler, however, refused to present Owens with his gold medal, saying "The Americans should be ashamed of themselves, letting Negroes win their medals for them. I shall not shake hands with this Negro."[2]

The legacy, or enduring memory, that Owens proved in Berlin was that achievement depends on the individual and not on his or her race or religion.

Secretary of State George C. Marshall developed the economic plan for Europe's economic recovery after World War II.

By almost any measure, World War II was the most expensive war in mankind's history. Defeating Hitler cost millions of lives and billions of dollars in property damage. In order to help Europe recover, the United States gave financial aid to its Allies while the countries of Eastern Europe languished under Soviet rule.

A New Kind of War

Although Europe was now at peace, the toll of the long war made it difficult for Germany and other countries to recover. It didn't help that relations between Stalin and the other Allied leaders had quickly soured once the war had ended. During a speech at Westminster College in Fulton, Missouri, in 1946, Winston Churchill lamented how the Soviets had isolated its satellite countries of Eastern Europe from the West.

"An Iron Curtain has descended across the continent. Behind that line lie all of the capitals of the ancient states of central and eastern Europe . . . all these famous cities and the populations around lie in the Soviet sphere and all are subject . . . to a very high and increasing measure of control from Moscow."[1]

Joseph Stalin responded angrily in a subsequent speech, saying that secure borders meant that the people were safer.

"The Soviet Union's loss of life [during World War II] has been several times greater than that of Britain and the United States of America put together. . . And so what can be so surprising about the fact that the Soviet Union, anxious for its future safety, is trying to see to it that governments loyal in their attitude to the Soviet Union should exist in these countries?"[2]

It was clear that Europe needed help to recover. And an economically healthy Europe was important for America, too. So in 1947, Secretary of State George C. Marshall gave a speech at Harvard University that outlined his plan to kick-start European recovery. The Marshall Plan, as it would become known, would give $20 million in relief to

European nations. Marshall explained, "The truth of the matter is that Europe's requirements for the next 3 or 4 years of foreign food and other essential products—principally from America—are so much greater than her present ability to pay that she must have substantial additional help, or face economic, social, and political deterioration of a very grave character. . . . The remedy lies in breaking the vicious circle and restoring the confidence of the European people in the economic future of their own countries and of Europe as a whole. The manufacturer and the farmer throughout wide areas must be able and willing to exchange their products for currencies the continuing value of which is not open to question."[3]

Marshall intended to include Eastern European countries, including the Soviet Union, in this relief effort as well. But the offer was thoroughly rejected by Stalin, who accused the U.S. of trying to trick the countries into accepting democracy. Ironically, American sentiment against the U.S.S.R. had become so negative that the plan might not have passed even if Stalin had accepted it.

By 1948, the Marshall plan was beginning to see results, especially in the Western part of Germany where France, Britain, and the U.S. introduced a new currency to help the economic recovery, which would also be used in West Berlin. In addition, Britain and the U.S. had already merged their zones in 1947 into a large sector they called Bizonia. It was administered by a council made up of Germans that was closely supervised by the Allies.

But in East Germany, the communist system installed by Stalin struggled, causing many hardships for the people living there. In an effort to promote socialism, a system in which the government controls industry, and wipe out capitalism, in which industry is owned privately by individuals, Stalin took away the right to own private property. Every aspect of life was controlled by the state.

Not only was Stalin frustrated by the East's inability to establish a strong economy, he was extremely upset that the Allies were laying the

groundwork for a united German state. In retaliation, he ordered a blockade of West Berlin, which cut that half of the city off from all land and
railway routes. According to the PBS program *The Race for the Superbomb,* Lucius Clay, the military governor of America's German zone ob-
served, "When the order of the Soviet Military Administration to close
all rail traffic from the western zones went into effect at 6:00 A.M. on the
morning of June 24, 1948, the three western sectors of Berlin, with a
civilian population of about 2,500,000 people, became dependent on
reserve stocks and airlift replacements. It was one of the most ruthless
efforts in modern times to use mass starvation for political coercion."[4]

President Truman immediately ordered a humanitarian airlift. For
over a year, planes flew around-the-clock missions to West Berlin carry-
ing food and supplies such as coal to its citizens, with planes landing at
three minutes intervals. In addition, soldiers protected the city's borders

*After Stalin
ordered the
blockade of West
Berlin, General
Lucius Clay
oversaw an around-
the-clock airlift
that is considered
one of the greatest
humanitarian
efforts in modern
history. Stalin was
protesting the Allies
plan to combine
their designated
zones into a new,
democratic
German Republic.*

Lucius Clay succeeded Dwight D. Eisenhower as Military Governor of Germany.

to prevent Stalin from trying to invade the city. The attempt to isolate West Berlin proved to be a humiliating failure for Stalin and, in May 1949, he called off the blockade. Eleven days later, the Western zones were combined into the Federal Republic of Germany. That August, the North American Treaty Organization, NATO, was formed between the United States, Canada, and the non-communist European countries. NATO countries pledged to help each other against any foreign aggression.

On September 23, 1949, President Truman announced that the Russians had successfully detonated their first atomic bomb. A month later, the German Democratic Republic was formed and East Berlin was named the new country's capital. The lines between East and West had been drawn and the boundary between the two formed the front line of what would come to be known as the Cold War. And Berlin was always the focal point of the escalating tensions between the U.S. and the Soviets.

Because of the hardships faced by the East Germans, many went to go live in West Germany. To make it harder for people to defect, the border between East and West Germany was ordered closed in May 1952. So instead, many Easy Germans traveled to East Berlin, where they could then walk into West Berlin. From there they could go to West Germany or anywhere else in Europe they wanted. Many of the people who left were skilled workers and professionals, which hurt the East German economy even more.

In April 1953, Stalin died. The official cause of death was a brain hemorrhage but some historians believe Stalin might have been murdered. There is some evidence that he was about to start another war. His goal was to conquer all of Europe and spread communism. But it was a war his advisors knew the Soviets could not win and could either destroy the U.S.S.R. or result in an atomic war, so to this day there remains speculation that Stalin was killed by members of his own government.

3

Stalin's successor was Nikita Khrushchev, who continued Stalin's Cold War policies. In response to the western Allies officially ending their occupation of Germany and Germany joining NATO, Khrushchev organized a military alliance among the Eastern European Soviet block countries that was called the Warsaw Pact. In 1958, he demanded that France, Britain, and the U.S. remove all troops from West Berlin. If they didn't, the unspoken threat was that he might invade the city and force the Allies out. For the next three years, the Soviets and the West held several conferences in an attempt to settle the issues over Berlin. None succeeded. And throughout that time, more and more East Germans continued to escape the repressive conditions by fleeing through Berlin.

The Cold War was even going on in space, as both East and West tried to be the first to send men into space, then land on the Moon. It was a far more peaceful situation than the arguments over the divided Berlin.

Krushchev's decision in 1962 to move atomic weapons into Cuba led to the Cuban Missile Crisis and brought the world to the brink of nuclear war. Eventually, Krushchev backed down and removed the weapons. Within a year, President Kennedy and Khrushchev signed the Nuclear Test Ban Treaty, the first ever disarmament agreement.

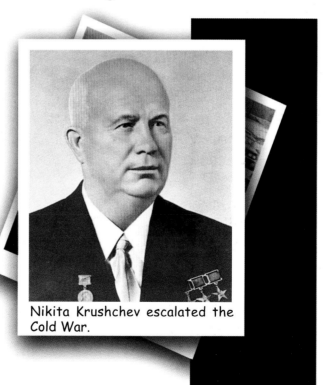

Nikita Krushchev escalated the Cold War.

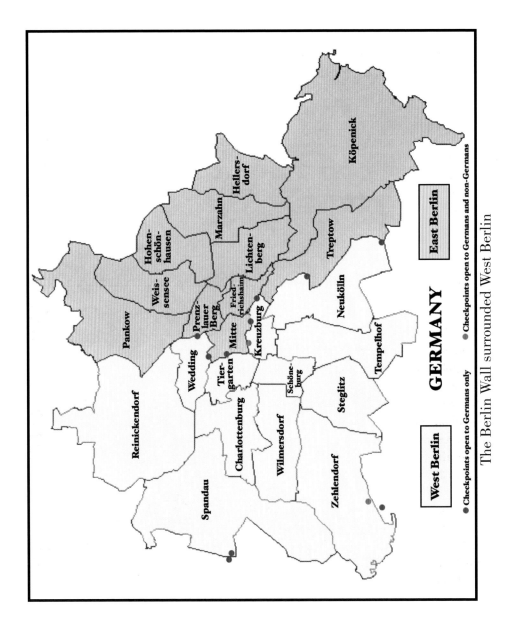

Köpenick

Hellers-
dorf

Marzahn

Hohen-
schön-
hausen

Treptow

Weis-
sensee

Lichten-
berg

Neukölln

Pankow

Fried-
richshain

Prenz-
lauer
Berg

Mitte

Kreuzburg

Wedding

Tier-
garten

Schöne-
burg

Tempelhof

Reinickendorf

Charlottenburg

Wilmersdorf

Steglitz

Spandau

Zehlendorf

GERMANY

West Berlin   East Berlin

● Checkpoints open to Germans only   ● Checkpoints open to Germans and non-Germans

The Berlin Wall surrounded West Berlin

FOR YOUR INFORMATION

By the time that U.S. President John F. Kennedy was elected in 1960, modern technology was rapidly advancing. It was a time of great inventiveness and ambition and Kennedy set a goal that up to then may have seemed like science fiction.

In a special message to Congress in 1961, Kennedy outlined his bold challenge to the American public.

"First, I believe that this nation should commit itself to achieving the goal, before this decade is out, of landing a man on the Moon and returning him safely to the Earth. No single space project in this period will be more impressive to mankind, or more important for the long-range exploration of space and none will be so difficult or expensive to accomplish. We propose to accelerate the development of the appropriate lunar space craft. We propose to develop alternate liquid and solid fuel boosters, much larger than any now being developed, until certain which is superior. We propose additional funds for other engine development and for unmanned explorations—explorations which are particularly important for one purpose which this nation will never overlook: the survival of the man who first makes this daring flight. But in a very real sense, it will not be one man going to the Moon—if we make this judgment affirmatively, it will be an entire nation. For all of us must work to put him there."[5]

Kennedy's grand vision succeeded in taking the Cold War into outer space. In 1957, the Soviets succeeded in launching the *Sputnik* satellite into space, and in 1961 Russian cosmonaut Yuri Gagarin became the first man in space. Believing it was important to catch up technologically, and as a matter of national pride, Kennedy came up with the lunar challenge after conferring with Vice President Lyndon Johnson.

Many people thought Kennedy was crazy. Instead he turned out to be prophetic. Although he would not live to see his dream fulfilled, on July 20, 1969, American astronaut Neil Armstrong would be the first human to walk on the moon.

Yuri Gagarin

There were over a hundred watchtowers along the border between East and West Germany.

In order to stop the mass exodus of people out of East Germany in the years after the end of World War II, Nikita Krushchev agreed for the border between East and West Berlin to be closed and enforced it with a show of military might.

The Iron Curtain

From 1949 to 1961 more than 2.6 million East Germans escaped to the West, which was 15 percent of the country's entire population. Walter Ulbricht, the East German leader, pleaded with Khrushchev to approve a radical plan to literally wall off the east from the west. When news of the plan leaked out, Ulbricht denied it. At an international press conference he commented, "I understand your question as follows: there are people in West Germany who want us to mobilize the construction workers of the GDR to build a wall. I am not aware of any such plans. . . . No one has the intention of constructing a wall."[1]

But in August of 1961 during a Communist Party meeting, Ulbricht got his wish. Two days after the meeting, Khrushchev announced in a radio broadcast that the "escape route" into the West had to be closed. Fearing what was to come, over 4,000 East Germans escaped that night.

The plan, called "Wall of China," outlined how the border between East and West Berlin would be closed. Within a few hours of the order, nearly all the crossing points had been closed. People living in houses close to the border were forced to evacuate so that a military zone could be set up on the border. The subway was halted and roadways that ran between the two sides of the city were closed and destroyed. Stone barricades were set up and tanks blocked checkpoints. Twenty-five miles of barbed wire was strung up to prevent passage. Within days, construction crews began to build a permanent wall to replace the temporary barriers.

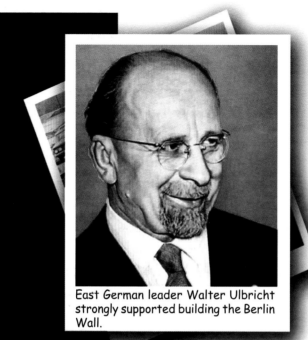

A founder of the German Communist party, Walter Ulbricht favored hard-line tactics to promote communism in East Germany and was a strong supporter of Soviet policies.

East German leader Walter Ulbricht strongly supported building the Berlin Wall.

The border between East and West Berlin and the two Germanys was over 100 miles long. To make sure nobody tried to sneak over, 25,000 armed guards were stationed along the east-west demarcation line every six feet in what was called the death area because a shoot to kill order was established for anyone trying to sneak across. Over the next 28 years, over 100 people would be killed. To prevent someone from trying to drive to freedom, a trench was dug. The area was also patrolled by watch dogs, and there were 116 watchtowers—32 in Berlin alone—as well as a second wall. Any East German citizen who wanted to visit either West Germany or West Berlin would need special government approval. And West Berliners were also restricted from entering the eastern half of the city.

Soviet Premier Nikita Khrushchev announced his approval for the Berlin Wall. He called it a wall to keep out wolves—the west.

For Berliners, the Wall tore their city in half and separated people from friends, family, and in many cases, their jobs. Interestingly, though, the Allies seemed to be calm about it. Although the barricades prevented East Germans from leaving, the construction of the wall did not affect the West's priorities, which were to keep allied troops in Berlin, the ability to get to West Berlin and the right of West Berliners to have self-rule.

Over time, the Wall was improved and made stronger and more impassible. It spanned Germany from the Baltic Sea to the border of Czechoslovakia and succeeded in effectively closing off East Germany. Interestingly, rather than be upset at their isolation, many young East Germans, who had grown up in the oppressive atmosphere and didn't know any other way of living, accepted the Wall and simply tried to make the best of things. But in other Soviet Block countries, people began to actively protest their lack of freedoms. Determined to keep tight control over Eastern Europe, the Soviets squashed these efforts to increase freedom with brutal military force.

The first country to try to exert reforms was Hungary under leader Imre Nagy. Nagy had been a loyal communist since World War I and he became involved in politics after World War II. Nagy's attitude began to change as he saw the violent tactics of hard line communists. An estimated 2,000 people were executed and another 100,000 imprisoned in the post-war years in an effort to eradicate, or wipe out, any opposition to communist rule. This caused Nagy to align himself with more moderate communists who still believed in the economic ideals of communism but believed individuals should have more personal freedoms.

After Stalin died, Nagy was made Hungary's prime minister and set about to reform the country's communist party. Hungary's previous Prime Minister, Matyas Rakosi, openly criticized Nagy and set out to ruin him by blaming Nagy for Hungary's serious economic problems. Like all Soviet controlled states, they suffered because of the tight controls placed on production by the government. Soon, Nagy was voted out

Hungary was the first Soviet block country to protest Soviet occupation and hard-line communist policies. Leader Imre Nagy supported communism but also promoted increased personal freedom for Hungarian citizens and free elections. For his efforts, Nagy was executed as a traitor.

Hungarian leader Imre Nagy sought social reforms.

as Prime Minister and Rakosi voted back in. Surprisingly, Khrushchev was not a supporter of Rakosi and a year later was forced out of office.

In October 1956, a group of students protested Soviet occupation and called for their country to adopt "true socialism." The police arrested some of the students and set off tear gas to break up the demonstration. When some of the students tried to free those who had been arrested, the police opened fire killing many of the students. The Hungarian people were horrified and the next day many Hungarian soldiers joined the students in protest. They tore down a statue of Stalin and chanted for the Russians to go home. Khrushchev responded by having tanks open fire on protesters, killing at least twelve.

In a surprise reversal, Hungary's Communist Party Central Committee reinstated Nagy as the country's leader. Nagy promised to promote personal freedom and a non-Soviet socialism aimed at improving

the lives of workers. This time, Nagy had the support of the Hungarian public, communist party, and newspapers. He gave mass media more freedom and encouraged the public to discuss how best to implement political and economic reforms. He released those who had been imprisoned for not being communists and promised to make sure everyone got their fair share of goods and services. Most upsetting to the Soviets, Nagy began planning to have free elections and withdrawing Hungary from the Warsaw Pact. He asked the United Nations for help in resolving their dispute with the Soviet Union and had Soviet troops withdrawn from Budapest.

Khrushchev could not allow such open defiance and on November 4, 1956, sent the Red Army to invade Budapest in a pre-dawn surprise attack. As the Soviet air force bombed the city, 1,000 tanks roared onto its streets. Soldiers stormed the Parliament and by day's end had captured Nagy and other members of his government. Khrushchev had Janos Kadar installed as the country's new leader and, on June 17, 1958, Imre Nagy was executed for treason.

Ten years later, a similar uprising took place in Czechoslovakia when another reformer tried to promote individual freedoms. Alexander Dubcek was determined to follow the will of his countrymen and established a more liberal kind of socialism where personal freedoms were allowed, which got the name "socialism with a human face." There was no censorship of the press and newspapers were allowed to openly criticize Russia. This was called the Prague Spring. But again, the Soviet leader, Leonid Brezhnev, could not tolerate this kind of liberation out of fear other countries under its control would want the same freedoms. Even though America was mired in the Vietnam War, the Soviets were still afraid the U.S. would try to challenge Soviet rule in Eastern Europe. So at dawn on August 20, 1968, armored vehicles and tanks rumbled through Prague as the Soviets and the other Warsaw Pact countries invaded. Dubcek was arrested along with other Czechoslovakian leaders. But unlike Nagy, Dubcek survived and was forced to publicly pledge

loyalty to Soviet communism and reverse any steps towards democracy that had been taken. He told the public the only way to ever go forward was to bend to the Soviet will—for now.

Dubcek would prove to be right. Although the Soviets won the battle over social reforms in Czechoslovakia, the movement started by Nagy and later Dubcek had quietly started to take root. Brezhnev's decision to invade a fellow communist country led many to mistrust him and caused many people throughout Eastern Europe to start questioning Soviet control and become increasingly uncomfortable with it. The seeds of democracy that had been sown in 1968 would finally begin to fully blossom twenty years later.

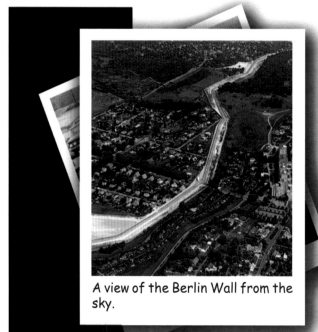

A view of the Berlin Wall from the sky.

The reform efforts by Imre Nagy and Alexander Dubcek sowed the seeds of the democratic movement that would bloom in the 1980s. Leonid Brezhnev's decision to invade Czechoslovakia would only increase the desire of Eastern Europeans to be free of Soviet rule.

FOR YOUR INFORMATION

While Eastern Europeans started to challenge Soviet political authority in the 1960s, the United States was going through its own revolution on a cultural level. During the 1950s, the U.S. was a mostly traditional country. The Baby Boomer generation—the 70 million children who were born during the post World War II years-grew up with a desire to move away from the strict social traditions of the 1950s and do things their own way. They wanted change. And spurred by the unpopularity of the Vietnam war, they instigated the biggest social revolution in American history.

The height of this cultural upheaval occurred in 1967 and 1968. The image most closely associated with the time is of "hippies" who grew long hair and beards—in direct defiance of the clean-cut images of the Eisenhower years. Psychedelic drug use was accepted among hippies who "turned on, tuned in and dropped out." San Francisco became the center of the "hippie movement" which spread a message of peace and free love. The term hippie was first used in a 1965 newspaper article written by Michael Fellon to describe the growing number of young bohemians, or people who do not conform to traditional social values. The term caught on and, on the July 7, 1967, *Time* magazine's cover story was "The Hippies: The Philosophy of a Subculture."

Hippies protesting

Even though hippies might be a quaint footnote in American history, the real force behind the cultural revolution were college students who protested the war and fought for social change. The turning point came in May 1970 when National Guard troops shot into a crowd of students at Kent State University who were protesting President Nixon's decision to expand the war in Southeast Asia by bombing Cambodia. Thirteen students were wounded and four were killed. The incident galvanized opponents of the war and caused many Americans to question government use of force.

The changes brought about in the 1960s continue to have far-reaching effects today. Besides the anti-war effort, many other social issues were stressed, including civil rights for African-Americans, women's rights, environmental issues, and personal freedoms. Many ideas which were considered revolutionary in the 1960s have become common ways of life today.

The Berlin Wall increasingly became the primary symbol of Soviet oppression.

In November 1989, the Berlin Wall was torn down and was the official end of Soviet rule. Friends and families separated nearly thrity years were reunited amid joyous scenes broadcast all over the world live on CNN. In the years since, portions of the wall have been restored and have become popular tourist attractions.

The Walls Come Tumbling Down

By the 1980s, it was becoming clear that the Soviet system of communism was not keeping up economically with democracy. There never seemed to be enough money. There were still buildings that had been destroyed during World War II that hadn't been rebuilt. In East Germany, many people lived in poverty, and even those who were able to find jobs were paid low wages. Making the citizens even more resentful was the fact that political leaders lived in luxury and seemed not to care about the average worker.

Despite the growing discontent, especially among East Berliners who could look across the barrier and see how much better life was on the West side of the Wall, East Germany's leader, Erich Honecher said, "The Berlin Wall will still exist in 50 and in 100 years unless the reasons for its existence are eliminated."[1] Little did he realize how wrong he was.

The truth was, the Soviet Union simply could not afford to keep the Cold War going. While America and other western nations flourished after World War II, Russia and the other Eastern Block countries did not. The life expectancy in the Soviet Union, especially among men, was markedly lower, and infant mortality, the death of babies, markedly higher than in the West. The U.S.S.R. had spent so much money on its military during the Cold War that there was little left for social and economic reforms. But it would take the amazing vision and courage of one man to set the wheels of democratic change in motion.

Mikhail Gorbachev was born into a peasant family and worked on their farm growing up while going to school. He knew first-hand the

hardships faced by the majority of people. He officially joined the Communist Party in 1952 and a year later graduated from Moscow University with a degree in law. Gorbachev was interested in politics and was eventually appointed the head of the agricultural department for the Stavropol region where he lived. Considered a rising political star, in 1971 he was elected to the Communist Central Committee and later became a member of the Politburo, which controlled the communist party.

When his close associate Yuri Andropov became the Communist Party's general secretary in 1982, Gorbachev's own power increased. Although Andropov was faithful to the Cold War, he also worked to improve the Soviet economy. But less than two years later, he died from kidney failure.

Andropov's successor, Konstantin Chernenko, was 72 and in failing health. But he continued his predecessor's attempts at reform and was an advocate for the government to invest more in agriculture and consumer goods. When Chernenko died in March 1985, his logical replacement was Mikhail Gorbachev, who introduced the policies of *glasnost* (openness) and *perestroika* (democratic reform). He knew from his experience in the agriculture department that the only way for the Soviet economy to improve was to weed out corruption, improve efficiency, and allow people more democratic choices. Most importantly, Gorbachev argued that it was time to end the arms race and the Cold War with the West. Although many people like to credit Ronald Reagan with pressuring Gorbachev to tear down the Berlin Wall, it was Gorbachev himself who set those wheels in motion. Not surprisingly, there were many in Gorbachev's own party who were appalled at the democratic reforms he was trying to institute. In part, members of the Central Committee and Politburo were worried their own influence and power would be lessened.

On Gorbachev's first official visit to West Germany in May 1989, he pledged that the U.S.S.R. would no longer use military force to prevent the Soviet satellite countries in Eastern Europe from pursuing democratic reforms. Almost immediately, the Hungarian government

Gorbachev instituted glastnost, a policy by which Eastern Block countries could free themselves from Soviet influence and establish independent governments. Within a short time, the Soviet Union also broke up into separate states. For successfully laying the foundation for the end of the Cold War, Gorbachev was awarded the 1990 Nobel Peace Prize.

Mikhail Gorbachev was instrumental in ending the Cold War.

announced it was opening its border with Austria starting in September. That resulted in a surge of East Germans pouring out of their country through Hungary and into the west in search of a better life. Within six months, almost a quarter million East Germans had defected.

As always, Berlin was the focal point. While West Berlin enjoyed prosperity, East Berliners suffered from lack of food, housing shortages, inadequate health care, and scarce products. Those East Germans who stayed formed peaceful opposition groups and demanded that East Germany and East Berlin be freed from occupation. Initially, the police responded violently but the number of protesters grew. October 7, 1989 was East Germany's 40th anniversary and resulted in a protest where over 1,000 people were arrested. On October 16, 1989, 120,000 demonstrators gathered, calling for free elections.

Feeling the growing pressure, Günter Schabowski, the leader of East Berlin's Communist Party known as the SED, agreed to review travel restrictions and entertain the possibility of new laws. On the evening of November 9, 1989, Schabowski announced that the border would be opened for "private trips abroad." Almost immediately, East Berliners stormed the Wall at the Brandenburg Gate and television cameras beamed live footage of the wild celebrations across the world. Those who were too impatient to go through the gate climbed the wall. People from West Berlin welcomed their fellow citizens from the East with embraces and tears as family and friends were reunited. After 28 years, the Berlin Wall had officially fallen.

The very next day, demolition of the Wall began and, by November 1990, the Wall was completely torn down, except for six segments intended to commemorate the day the Wall fell. The concrete blocks that once made up the wall were crushed and used to make roads and other improvements, and others were auctioned off to raise money. In July 1990, an economic, monetary, and social union between East and West Germany was formed, effectively reuniting Germany under one flag.

Throughout Eastern Europe Gorbachev's policy of *glastnost* allowed for Eastern European countries to peacefully break away from Soviet influence and interference. One after another, like dominoes falling, countries voted out their communist leaders and installed more socially democratic governments. Many historians have pointed out that never in recorded history has the dissolution of an empire taken place so peacefully as Gorbachev kept his promise that there would be no military intervention.

Even so, many of Gorbachev's critics saw this as unacceptable, especially when it caused many of the Soviet republics to start demonstrating for independence as well. In 1991, while Gorbachev was on vacation, hard-liners who did not want the Soviet Union to break up into independent states staged an attempted coup, or takeover. It was a tense

few days as the world waited and watched to see if all the reforms instituted by Gorbachev would be reversed.

But the coup failed, partly because it did not have the support of the military and because of massive public protests against it. After the attempted coup, Gorbachev was forced to resign because there was no longer a Soviet Union to rule over. All the power was effectively transferred to the leaders of the various Soviet states, the largest of which is Russia, which accounted for 75 percent of the former U.S.S.R. For his part in skillfully dismantling the Cold War, Mikhail Gorbachev would be awarded the 1990 Nobel Peace Prize.

Today, all that remains of the Wall itself are a few commemorative pieces, while its former location is designated by a red line or twin rows of cobblestones. But the Berlin Wall will forever remain a symbol of both repression and the power of the human spirit striving for freedom.

Alexandra Hildebrandt, art historian and director of a private museum located near the location of Checkpoint Charley, erected 1,065 crosses that bear the names of people killed in East Germany, both over the wall and in other locations. In 2005, a judge ordered the crosses removed at the request of the bank that currently owns the property.

Eight foot tall wooden crosses honoring those who died trying to flee East Germany were erected as a memorial near the Berlin Wall.

In East Berlin, in addition to not having the ability to freely come and go out of the country as you wanted, people couldn't afford to buy many of the things those living in the Western democracies took for granted. As the economic conditions worsened in East Germany, many people in East Berlin grew bitter, knowing that just on the other side of the wall West Berlin was thriving thanks to the support of the United States and the other Allies.

Something that seems relatively unimportant became the symbol of everything that was wrong in East Berlin—and might even have led to the crumbling of the Wall back in the 1970s. It can be argued that the most popular drink in both East and West Germany is coffee. What makes that surprising is that as recently as World War II, coffee was considered a luxury item, with only the wealthier citizens able to afford to drink it on a daily basis.

But after the end of the war, coffee became available for all Germans, rich and poor, and its popularity soared. From the early 1970s to the end of the decade, the price of imported coffee steadily rose until there was a huge jump in price in 1976, making it four times as expensive as it had been previously. Because of East Germany's severe financial problems, the government could not afford to import enough coffee to fill the demand.

Milchkaffee

So during the summer of 1977 the Politburo, which was the main governing organization of the Soviet Communist Party, ordered that the cheaper brands of coffee be removed from stores and stopped paying for coffee to be served in government offices. Instead, the government introduced a new kind of coffee blend, called Milchkaffee (mixed coffee) that was half coffee and half a variety of other ingredients including sugar beet, rye, and chicory. This only made matters worse because it tasted terrible, creating anger and resentment among East Berliners. The situation became known as the "coffee crisis" and came to symbolize the difficulties of living under the Soviet's communist regime.

Fortunately, by the following year coffee prices began to go back down and East Germany could again afford to import coffee. The "coffee crisis" ended for good when the Wall came down.

Chronology

1945	World War II ends; Yalta Conference divides Germany and its capital, Berlin, into four zones controlled by the Soviets, France, Britain and the United States.
1946	An official pass is required to travel between Germany's sectors.
1948	The Soviets begin the blockade of Berlin, resulting in the Berlin Airlift.
1949	Soviets end blockade; German Democratic Republic, known as East Germany, is established.
1952	The border between East and West Germany is closed.
1953	Soviets use military force to suppress workers' revolt.
1955	West Germany joins NATO.
1957	East Germans face prosecution for leaving the country without government permission.
1961	Barriers are built dividing East and West Berlin.
1962	The Cuban Missile Crisis brings the world to the brink of nuclear war.
1963	President John Kennedy visits Berlin; West Berliners are allowed to visit the eastern sector of the city for the first time in two years.
1964	Fifty-seven people escape under the wall using a 470° tunnel.
1968	Soviet Union sends troops and tanks to crush Prague Spring.
1972	The United States and Russia sign biological weapons ban treaty; Nixon visits Moscow.
1985	Newly elected Soviet leader Mikhail Gorbachev begins democratic reform.
1987	President Reagan challenges Gorbachev to tear down Berlin Wall.
1989	Citizens tear down Berlin Wall.
1990	Germany is reunited into one country.
1991	The Soviet Union officially dissolves.
1997	A red line is painted to mark where the Berlin Wall once stood.
2003	A monument is dedicated to Chris Gueffroy.
2005	The Berlin Wall Museum remains a popular tourist destination.

Timeline in History

1914	Archduke Ferdinand is assassinated
1918	Russia's Czar Nicholas II and his family are murdered
1933	Hitler becomes German Chancellor
1942	The Battle of Stalingrad
1945	VE Day; United Nations founded
1949	Canada, the United States, and the western European countries establish NATO
1950	Senator Joseph McCarthy launches anti-Communism crusade
1951	Julius and Ethel Rosenberg convicted of espionage on behalf of Soviets
1954	United States tests Hydrogen bomb on Bikini atoll in Pacific
1955	Communist countries sign Warsaw Pact
1956	Soviets crush Hungarian revolt
1960	United States spy plane pilot captured by Soviets
1961	Yuri Gagarin becomes first man in space
1962	Cuban missile crisis has world on brink of atomic war
1965	The Soviet Union offers weapons and financial assistance to North Vietnam
1968	Soviets invade Czechoslovakia
1973	East and West Germany establish diplomatic ties
1975	The Vietnam War ends
1977	Soviet troops enter Afghanistan
1979	Pope John Paul II visits Poland
1984	Soviets boycott summer Olympics held in Los Angeles
1986	Nuclear Reactor in Chernobyl explodes
1987	U.S. and Soviets agree to destroy nuclear warheads
1990	Mikhail Gorbachev wins Nobel Peace Prize; Hungary holds first free elections
1991	Warsaw Pact is officially dissolved
1994	Chechnya engages in Civil War with Russia
1999	European Union establishes formal policy with Russia
2000	Vladimir Putin elected Russian president; Russia and the United States announce new agreement on strategic nuclear weapons reduction
2001	The United States bombs Afghanistan
2002	Russia becomes ally of NATO
2005	Chechen separatist leader Aslan Maskhadov reportedly killed by Russian forces

Chapter Notes

Chapter 1   The Quest for Freedom

1. MSNBC, Andy Eckardt, *Victims of the Berlin Wall Never Forgotten*—http://www.msnbc.com/id/6470285

Chapter 2   Rebuilding

1. Truman, Harry S. *Year of Decisions* (Garden City, NY: Doubleday and Company, 1955) p. 416.

2. Phil Taylor, "Flying in the Face of the Fuhrer: August 3–9 1936, Jesse Owens Dominates the Berlin Olympics," *Sports Illustrated*, November 29, 1999.

Chapter 3   A New Kind of War

1. Churchill's Speech at Westminster can be found at several sites online, including http://www.cnn.com/SPECIALS/cold.war/episodes/02/documents/churchill/

2. http://www.ne'wseum.org/cybernewseum/exhibits/berlin_wall/iron.htm

3. http://usinfo.state.gov/usa/infousa/facts/democrac/57.htm

4. PBS' *Race for the Superbomb*.

5. www.cnn.com

Chapter 4   The Iron Curtain

1. http://t3.preservice.org/T0110200/bwall.html

2. http://www.newseum.org/cybernewseum/exhibits/berlin_wall/iron.htm

Chapter 5   The Walls Come Tumbling Down

1. http://www.newseum.org/cybernewseum/exhibits/berlin_wall/iron.htm

Glossary

blockade (block-AID)
To prevent access to a place or country by means of military force.

capitalism (KAP-I-talh-ism)
A free economy driven by private ownership.

convene (kun-VEEN)
An official order to meet as a group.

coup (koo)
To change a government by force.

defect (duh-FECT)
To leave a place because of political beliefs and go live somewhere else.

deforestation (dee-for-ess-STAY-shun)
The destruction of forest through cutting, burning or other damage.

glasnost (GLASS-knowst)
A soviet policy that allowed open discussion of social issues.

license (LIE-sense)
A legal agreement that gives someone permission to use a brand, such as Pac-Man, for certain purposes or under certain conditions.

perestroika (pair-eh-STROYK-uh)
A Soviet economic policy intended to increase efficiency.

socialism (SO-shall-ism)
When the government, instead of private industry, controls products and services.

totalitarian (toe-tal-I-TAIR-ee-an)
A government that does not allow opposing view points.

For Further Reading

For Young Adults

Epler, Doris. *The Berlin Wall; How It Rose And Why It Fell*. New Milford, CT: Millbrook Press, 1992.

Grant, R.G. *The Berlin Wall*. Austin, TX: Raintree Steck-Vaughn Publishers, 1998.

Degens, T. *Freya on the Wall*. San Diego, CA: Browndeer Press, 1997.

Works Consulted

Botting, Douglas. *From the Ruins of the Reich: Germany 1945–1949*. New York: New American Library, 1985.

"East Germans Close Berlin Border," *Associated Press*, August 13, 1961.

Garden, Nancy. *Berlin: City Split in Two*. New York: Putnam, 1971.

MacCloskey, Monro. *The Infamous Wall of Berlin*. New York: Richards Rosen Press, 1967.

Starcevic, Nesha. "East Germany Opens Borders, Revelers Dance Atop Berlin Wall," *Associated Press*, November 9, 1989.

Truman, Harry S. *Year of Decisions*. Garden City, NY: Doubleday and Company, 1955.

Williams, Carol J., "1 Million East Germans Visit the West in One Day," *Associated Press*, November 11, 1989.

Wyden, Peter. *Wall: The Inside Story of Divided Berlin*. New York: Simon and Schuster, 1989.

On the Internet

http://www.dailysoft.com/berlinwall/

http://www.wall-berlin.org/gb/berlin.htm

http://www.newseum.org/berlinwall/

http://t3.preservice.org/T0110200/bwall.html

"Berlin," http://encarta.msn.com/encyclopedia_761570640/Berlin.html

"Berlin Wall," http://encarta.msn.com/encyclopedia_761580628/Berlin_Wall.html

www.cnn.com/SPECIALS/cold.war/episodes/02/documents/churchill/

History Channel
www.historychannel.com

History and Politics Outloud
www.hpol.org/transcript.php?id=12.

Newseum: Berlin Wall
www.newseum.org/cybernewseum/exhibits/berlin_wall/iron.htm

USIA
www.usinfo.state.gov/usa/infousa/facts/democrac/57.htm

Race for the Superbomb
www.PBS.org

Index

DUE DATE
